Fish

Revised and updated

Rod Theodorou

Heinemann
LIBRARY

www.heinemann.co.uk/library
Visit our website to find out more information about Heinemann Library books.

To order:
☎ Phone 44 (0) 1865 888066
Send a fax to 44 (0) 1865 314091
Visit the Heinemann Bookshop at www.heinemann.co.uk/library to browse our
catalogue and order online.

First published in Great Britain by Heinemann Library,
Halley Court, Jordan Hill, Oxford OX2 8EJ, part
of Harcourt Education. Heinemann is a registered
trademark of Harcourt Education Ltd.

Editorial: Clare Lewis
Design: Joanna Hinton-Malivoire
Illustration: Barry Atkinson Illustration
Picture research: Ruth Blair
Production: Sevy Ribierre

Printed and bound in China by South
China Printing Co. Ltd.

10-digit ISBN 0 431 93234 4
13-digit ISBN 978 0 431 93234 7
11 10 09 08 07
10 9 8 7 6 5 4 3 2 1

British Library Cataloguing in Publication Data
Theodorou, Rod
Animal Young: Fish - 2nd edition
597.1'39
A full catalogue record for this book is available from
the British Library.

Acknowledgements
The publishers would like to thank the following for
permission to reproduce photographs:
Ardea London Ltd p. **13**, Kurt Amsler p. **5**; BBC: Jeff
Foott p. **15**; Bruce Coleman: Pacific Stock p. **7**, Charles
& Sandra Hood p. **16**, Jane Burton p. **22**, Pacific
Stock p. **7**; Creatas p. **4** bottom left; Digital Stock p.
4 top right and middle left; Digital Vision p. **4** bottom
right; FLPA: Phil McLean p. **17**, Steve McCutcheon
p. **9**; Nature P L: Doug Perrine p. **18**; Getty Images /
Photodisc p. **4** top left and middle right; NHPA: Norbert
Wu p. **12**; OSF: Keith Ringland p. **6**, David Thompson
p. **8**, David B Fleetham p. **10**, Zig Leszczynski p. **11**,
Mark Deeble & Victoria Stone p. **14**, Rudie Kuiter p. **20**,
Peter Parks p. **23**, Jeff Foott p. **24**, Rodger Jackman p.
25; Planet Earth: Peter Scoones p. **21**; Tony Stone: Fred
Bavendam p. **30**, Marc Chamberlain p. **19**.

Cover photograph of orange fish reproduced with
permission of Corbis/Warren Morgan.

Every effort has been made to contact copyright holders
of any material reproduced in this book. Any omissions
will be rectified in subsequent printings if notice is given
to the publishers.

Contents

Some words are shown in bold, **like this**. You can find out what they mean by looking in the Glossary.

Introduction

There are many different types of animals. All animals have babies. They look after their babies in different ways.

These are the six main animal groups.

Mammal   Bird

Amphibian  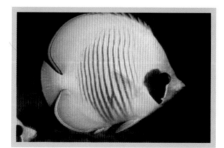 Fish

Reptile   Insect

Fish can be lots of different shapes, sizes, and colours.

This book is about fish. Fish live in ponds, lakes, rivers, and seas all over the world. There are lots of different types of fish.

What is a fish?

All fish:

- live in water
- breathe **oxygen** with their **gills**
- swim using their **fins**.

Salmon

fins

gills

scales

tail fin

Most fish:

- have hard **scales** on their body
- lay eggs that **hatch** into baby fish.

Eels are fish but most do not have scales.
Their bodies are soft and smooth.

Making a nest

Most fish do not make nests. They lay their eggs in the water and swim away. Some fish make a nest for their eggs. The nest keeps the eggs safe.

Sticklebacks make a little cave out of weeds on the **riverbed**.

This female salmon digs a nest and then covers her eggs with gravel to keep them safe.

Fish make their nests at the bottom of rivers or at the **seabed**. They scoop out a hole in the sand with their bodies. Some even push weeds into their nests.

Protecting the nest

Some fish stay close to their nests. They guard their eggs or baby fish from **predators**. They attack any other animal that comes near the nest.

This triggerfish will attack anything that comes near his eggs – even divers!

Eggs are laid by female fish, but it is often the male fish that looks after them. He may go for days without food just to protect the eggs.

When the two-metre-long African lungfish is protecting his nest, other fish stay away!

Eggs

Most fish lay thousands, or even millions, of eggs. The eggs are usually tiny and round. They do not have hard shells and are easily eaten by other animals.

When this ocean sunfish grows up it will be able to lay over 5 million eggs at once!

This baby dogfish shark grows inside an egg case.

egg case

baby shark

Other fish lay hard egg cases shaped like a purse. They have a curly leg at each corner that hooks onto seaweed. The eggs stay there until the babies **hatch**.

Fish Fry

When baby fish **hatch** from eggs they are called **fry** or larvae. They are often only a few millimetres long. They do not look much like their parents yet.

fish fry

Tiny fish fry like these emperor cichlid fry are very hard for **predators** to spot.

salmon fry

yolk sac

This salmon fry stays hidden in gravel for weeks, living off its yolk sac.

Some fry have a bag growing under their stomachs. It is called a **yolk sac**. The fry do not need to go hunting. They can live for weeks off the food in their yolk sacs.

Staying safe

When millions of fish eggs **hatch** into millions of fish **fry**, they attract lots of **predators**. Other fish, shrimps, crabs, and jellyfish eat huge numbers of fry.

This Dover sole has attacked a fish fry.

These red devil fry are hiding among rocks on the seabed.

Fish fry try to stay hidden from predators. Some hide near the **seabed** amongst rocks or weeds. Others swim next to floating weeds at the surface.

Live birth

Some sharks and other fish do not lay eggs.
Their babies grow inside them and are born
alive. The babies are born strong and ready
to catch their own food.

This baby shark has just been born.

young stingray

Stingrays give birth to live young.

Fish that give birth to live young only have a few babies at a time. Their babies are much harder for **predators** to catch and eat than tiny fish **fry**.

Looking after the young

Most fish do not look after their young.
A few kinds of fish do stay close to their
young and protect them.

Male seahorses have a special **pouch** where the female lays her eggs. The young **hatch** out from the pouch.

baby seahorse

pouch

If they are in danger these cichlid fry swim into their mothers' mouths.

Some kinds of fish look after their **fry** in their mouths! They suck up their eggs and fry and keep them safe in their mouths.

Growing up

As fish fry grow up, their **yolk sacs** disappear. They have to find their own food. They feed on **plankton** and other tiny water creatures.

These jewel cichlid **fry** are looking for food on the **seabed**.

Young fish often swim together in large groups called shoals or schools. They are safer in a shoal. When a big fish attacks a shoal it cannot decide which fish to chase.

This shoal contains thousands of young fry.

Amazing journeys

Some fish do not spend all their lives in the same place. Instead they **migrate** huge distances.

Salmon **fry** live in rivers for two years. Then they swim to the sea. When they are older they swim back up the river to breed.

These young eels swim across the ocean to live in rivers. Years later they swim back to the sea to breed.

Migrating fish may take two or three years to reach the sea or river where they **breed**. Once they have laid their eggs they usually die.

Fish life cycles

This is how a baby nurse shark is born.
The baby shark looks a lot like its mother.

4. The young shark grows bigger. It becomes an adult.

1. The baby shark grows inside its mother.

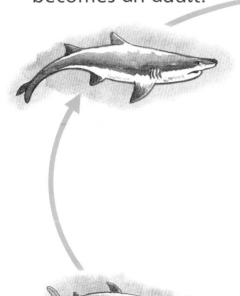

3. The baby swims off to find its own food.

2. The baby is born alive.

This is how a sole (called a flatfish) hatches and grows up. The sole **fry** does not look much like its mother.

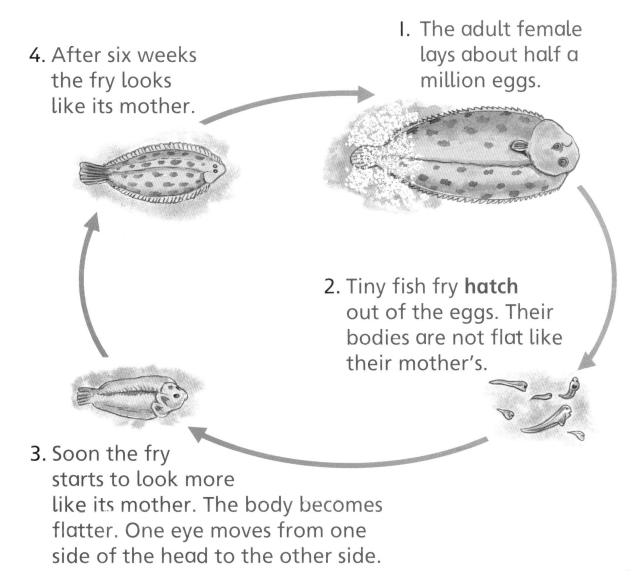

4. After six weeks the fry looks like its mother.

1. The adult female lays about half a million eggs.

2. Tiny fish fry **hatch** out of the eggs. Their bodies are not flat like their mother's.

3. Soon the fry starts to look more like its mother. The body becomes flatter. One eye moves from one side of the head to the other side.

Fish and other animals

		FISH	
WHAT THEY LOOK LIKE:	Bones inside body	all	
	Number of legs	none	
	Hair on body	none	
	Scaly skin	most	
	Wings	none	
	Feathers	none	
WHERE THEY LIVE:	On land	none	
	In water	all	
HOW THEY ARE BORN:	Grows babies inside body	some	
	Lays eggs	most	
HOW THEY FEED YOUNG:	Feeds baby milk	none	
	Brings baby food	none	

 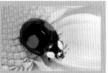   

MAMMALS	INSECTS	AMPHIBIANS	BIRDS	REPTILES
all	none	all	all	all
none, 2, or 4	6	4 or none	2	4 or none
all	all	none	none	none
few	none	none	none	all
some	most	none	all	none
none	none	none	all	none
most	most	most	all	most
some	some	some	none	some
most	some	few	none	some
few	most	most	all	most
all	none	none	none	none
most	some	none	most	none

Fantastic fish!

- The smallest fish is the tiny goby. An adult goby is only as long as your thumbnail.

- Some fish only live for a few weeks. Fish called sturgeons can live for 50 years.

- Puffer fish have a good way of scaring enemies. They take in lots of water and puff up into a spiny ball.

- The biggest fish is the whale shark. It can grow 15 metres (50 feet) long.

Whale shark

Glossary

breed a male and a female come together to make babies

fin flat part of a fish's body that helps it to swim or turn

fry very small, young fish

gill part of a fish's body that takes oxygen from water to help it breathe

hatch to be born from an egg

migrate to move from one place to another each year

oxygen a gas that all animals and plants need to breathe in order to live

plankton tiny animals and plants that live in the sea

pouch pocket of skin on the stomach of some animals in which their babies grow

predator an animal that hunts and kills other animals for food

riverbed the ground at the bottom of a river

scales small, flat pieces of hard skin that cover a fish's body

seabed the ground at the bottom of the sea

yolk sac a bag of food that is part of some baby fish and which they can eat after they are born

Find out more

Books

A Pet's Life: Goldfish, Anita Ganeri (Heinemann Library, 2003)

From Egg to Adult: The Life Cycle of a Fish, Louise & Richard Spilsbury (Heinemann Library, 2003)

Wild World: Watching Sharks in the Oceans, L. Patricia Kite (Heinemann Library, 2006)

Website

www.nefsc.noaa.gov/faq/

Index

Titles in the *Animal Young* series include:

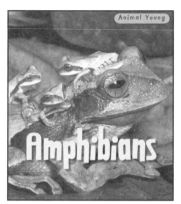

Hardback   978-0-431-93232-3

Hardback   978-0-431-93233-0

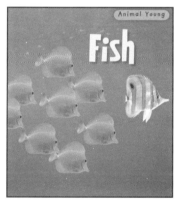

Hardback   978-0-431-93234-7

Hardback   978-0-431-93235-4

Hardback   978-0-431-93236-1

Hardback   978-0-431-93237-8

Find out about other titles from Heinemann Library on our website www.heinemann.co.uk/library